THE POWER OF IDEAS

A Practical Guide to Spark Your Creativity,
Activate Potential, Drive Success, and
Transform Your Life.

PRADIP DAS

© **Copyright 2024 - All rights reserved.**

The content contained within this book may not be reproduced, duplicated, or transmitted without direct written permission from the author or the publisher. Under no circumstances will any blame or legal responsibility be held against the publisher, or author, for any damages, reparation, or monetary loss due to the information contained within this book. Either directly or indirectly.

Legal Notice:
This book is copyright protected. This book is only for personal use. You cannot amend, distribute, sell, use, quote or paraphrase any part, or the content within this book, without the consent of the author or publisher.

Disclaimer Notice:
Please note the information contained within this document is for educational and entertainment purposes only. All effort has been executed to present accurate, up to date, and reliable, complete information. No warranties of any kind are declared or implied.

Readers acknowledge that the author is not engaging in the rendering of legal, financial, medical or professional advice. The content within this book has been derived from various sources. Please consult a licensed professional before attempting any techniques outlined in this book.

By reading this document, the reader agrees that under no circumstances is the author responsible for any losses, direct or indirect, which are incurred as a result of the use of information contained within this document, including, but not limited to, — errors, omissions, or inaccuracies.

Author Profile

Table of Contents

Table of Contents 4

Introduction 5

Power of Ideas 8

Unleashing Your Potential 12

Creative Mind Mastery 18

Secrets of Creativity 25

Idea Power 31

Idea Generation Techniques 42

Developing Ideas 48

Applying Ideas 53

Daily Implementation 58

Impactful Ideas 63

Life-Changing Ideas 68

Business-Leveraging Ideas 78

Conclusion 84

Introduction

Have you ever wondered how a simple thought, a momentary spark of inspiration, can ignite a revolution, change the course of history, or transform the way we live? Prepare to explore the extraordinary impact that ideas have on our lives and our world.

Against all odds, Albert Einstein, whose idea of relativity transformed our understanding of space, time, and the universe itself, defied convention and reshaped the very fabric of reality with his groundbreaking theories.

Despite facing countless obstacles as a woman in a male-dominated field, Marie Curie's relentless pursuit of knowledge led to groundbreaking advancements in radioactivity. Her insatiable curiosity and unwavering determination paved the way for scientific breakthroughs that continue to shape our world today.

Steve Jobs, the co-founder of Apple Inc. started in a garage and built one of the most influential tech companies in the world. His vision for personal computing and later, for devices like the iPhone, revolutionized the way we live, work, and communicate.

These stories remind us of the incredible power of ideas to transcend boundaries, defy expectations, and change lives. But you don't have to be a genius or a Nobel laureate to make an impact. Each of us has the potential to be a catalyst for change, to spark innovation, and to make a difference in the world around us.

In this book, we'll explore the principles of creativity, innovation, and problem-solving that drive the power of ideas. We'll uncover how ideas are born, nurtured, and brought to life, and we'll learn how to unlock our full potential to shape a brighter future for ourselves and others.

So, dear reader, are you ready to unleash the power of your ideas? Are you ready to challenge convention, push the boundaries of what's possible, and leave your mark on the world? The journey begins now. Let's discover the limitless potential of "The Power of Ideas."

Power of Ideas

A single idea can revolutionize an industry, create a successful business, or transform a life. Here are some real-life examples from the business world that highlight the extraordinary impact of a single idea:

Steve Jobs and the iPhone

Idea: Combining a phone, an iPod, and an internet communicator into one device.

Impact: The iPhone revolutionized the smartphone industry, making Apple one of the most valuable companies in the world. It transformed how we communicate, work, and entertain ourselves.

Jeff Bezos and Amazon

Idea: Creating an online bookstore that could offer more titles than any physical store.

Impact: Amazon started as an online bookstore but expanded into a global e-commerce giant. It redefined the retail industry and introduced innovations like one-click shopping and same-day delivery.

Elon Musk and Tesla

Idea: Producing electric vehicles that are desirable and affordable for the mass market.

Impact: Tesla accelerated the world's transition to sustainable energy, becoming a leader in the electric vehicle market and spurring other automakers to focus on electric cars.

Howard Schultz and Starbucks

Idea: Bringing the Italian coffeehouse culture to the United States.

Impact: Starbucks created a new coffee culture, turning coffee shops into social hubs.

It expanded globally, influencing how people enjoy coffee and interact socially.

Imagine a world where a single idea has the power to change everything. It's not just any idea—it's an idea that sparks a revolution, transforms lives, and shapes the course of history. This is the power of ideas.

But what exactly is an idea? It's more than just a thought; it's a spark of inspiration, a flash of insight that ignites our imagination and propels us forward. Ideas have the power to challenge the status quo, disrupt the norm, and push the boundaries of what's possible.

Every great invention, every groundbreaking discovery, every monumental achievement began as an idea in someone's mind. From the wheel to the internet, from democracy to human rights, ideas have shaped the world we live in and continue to drive progress and innovation.

But the power of ideas goes beyond just changing the world; it also has the power to change us. Ideas can inspire us to dream bigger, think differently, and believe in ourselves and our potential. They can challenge our beliefs, broaden our horizons, and open our minds to new possibilities.

So, the next time you have an idea—no matter how big or small—don't underestimate its power. Nurture it, cultivate it, and let it guide you on a journey of exploration and discovery. Who knows? Your idea could be the next big thing, the spark that sets the world on fire and transforms lives for generations to come.

Unleashing Your Potential

There exists a force so potent, so transformative, that it has the power to shape the course of history and ignite revolutions. This force is none other than the humble idea—the seed of innovation, the spark of creativity, and the catalyst for change. But what is the essence of ideas? What makes them so powerful, so charismatic, and so essential to the human experience?

At their core, ideas are more than just fleeting thoughts or passing musings. They are the building blocks of our reality, the foundation upon which civilizations rise and fall. Every invention, every discovery, every masterpiece—these are all born from the fertile soil of human imagination, nurtured by the relentless pursuit of progress and fueled by the desire to leave a mark on the world.

But ideas are not just abstract concepts floating in the ether; they are living, breathing entities with the power to shape our perceptions, our beliefs, and our actions. They have the ability to challenge the status quo, disrupt the norm, and inspire individuals to reach beyond the confines of their limitations. Ideas are the whispers of possibility in a world filled with uncertainty, the guiding lights that lead us toward a brighter tomorrow.

Yet, for all their potential, ideas are fragile things, easily lost in the chaos of everyday life or drowned out by the noise of doubt and skepticism. It is up to us, as stewards of creativity and champions of innovation, to nurture and protect these precious seeds of inspiration, to cultivate them with care and attention, and to bring them to fruition through action and perseverance.

So, the next time you find yourself lost in thought, pondering the mysteries of the universe or dreaming of a better world, remember the essence of ideas—their power to transform, to uplift, and to illuminate the path forward. For in the fertile soil of your imagination lies the potential to change the world, one idea at a time.

Ideas. They're like tiny sparks that ignite the fires of innovation, creativity, and change. But what exactly are ideas, and where do they come from?

Exploring the Nature of Ideas

Close your eyes for a moment and imagine a world without ideas. It's a bleak and barren landscape, devoid of progress, discovery, and invention. Ideas are the lifeblood of human civilization, the driving force behind every breakthrough, every discovery, and every advancement we've ever made.

But what are ideas, really? They're more than just random thoughts floating around in our heads. Ideas are the seeds of possibility, the blueprints for change, and the catalysts for transformation. They can come to us in moments of inspiration, in flashes of insight, or through hours of deliberate brainstorming and reflection.

Think about the last time you had a great idea. Maybe it was a solution to a problem at work, a new recipe to try in the kitchen, or a vision for a creative project. How did it feel? Did you feel a surge of excitement, a sense of clarity, a burst of energy? That's the power of ideas at work, igniting your imagination and propelling you forward.

Impact of Ideas

From the wheel to the internet, from democracy to human rights, ideas have shaped the course of civilization in profound and lasting ways.

Think about some of the greatest ideas in history. The idea of democracy, born in ancient Greece, revolutionized the way societies are governed and laid the foundation for modern governance. The idea of the scientific method, developed during the Renaissance, transformed our understanding of the natural world and paved the way for countless scientific discoveries.

But ideas don't just shape the big events of history; they also shape our everyday lives in subtle and meaningful ways. The idea of kindness, for example, has the power to brighten someone's day and change the course of their life. The idea of forgiveness has the power to heal wounds and mend broken relationships.

Let's cherish the ideas that have shaped our past and work on the ideas that will shape our future. And let's never underestimate the potential of a single idea to change the world.

Creative Mind Mastery

Have you ever wondered where ideas come from? Why do some people seem to have an endless supply of them, while others struggle to come up with even one? The answer lies in the fascinating realm of the psychology of ideas—a realm where the mind's creative potential is unlocked, and the seeds of innovation are planted.

At its core, the psychology of ideas is about understanding how our minds work when it comes to generating, nurturing, and developing new thoughts and concepts. It's about exploring the cognitive processes that underpin creativity and innovation, and uncovering the secrets of the creative mind.

One of the key insights from the psychology of ideas is that creativity is not a rare gift bestowed upon a select few; rather, it's a fundamental aspect of human nature that resides within each and every one of us. Think about it: from the moment we're born, our minds are constantly at work, making connections, forming associations, and generating new possibilities. It's what allows us to solve problems, adapt to new situations, and imagine a better future.

While we all have the capacity for creativity, not all of us know how to tap into it effectively. That's where the psychology of ideas comes in. By understanding the factors that influence creativity—such as mindset, environment, and motivation—we can learn to harness our creative potential and unleash a torrent of innovative thinking.

So, how do we unlock the mind's creative potential? It starts with cultivating the right mindset—a mindset of curiosity, openness, and experimentation. It means facing uncertainty and being willing to take risks, knowing that failure is not the end but rather a stepping stone on the path to success. It means surrounding ourselves with diverse perspectives and experiences, and seeking out new ideas and inspiration wherever we can find them.

But perhaps most importantly, unlocking the mind's creative potential means giving ourselves permission to dream—to dream big, to dream boldly, and to dream without limits. Because it's in those moments of uncontrolled imagination that the seeds of truly groundbreaking ideas are planted, waiting to take root and flourish in the fertile soil of our minds.

So, as you move on your journey into the psychology of ideas, I encourage you to adopt the unknown, to embrace the possibilities, and to accept the power of your own creativity. For in doing so, you'll not only unlock the secrets of the creative mind but also unleash a force that has the power to transform your life—and the world—forever.

Understanding How Ideas Shape Perception"

Have you ever stopped to consider the mysterious ways in which ideas shape our perception of the world? It's a fascinating journey into the depths of the human mind, where the seeds of creativity are planted, and the landscape of reality is forever altered.

Our perception is like a canvas, and ideas are the paintbrushes that color our experiences. From the moment we're born, we're bombarded with a myriad of ideas—from the stories we're told to the images we see to the beliefs we hold dear. These ideas become the building blocks of our reality, shaping our thoughts, feelings, and actions in profound ways.

But how do these ideas take root in our minds, and what drives the process of idea generation? It's a complex interplay of cognitive processes that unfolds within the recesses of our brains. From the initial spark of inspiration to the moment of realization, idea generation is a journey of exploration, discovery, and synthesis. It's a dance between our conscious and subconscious minds, where creativity flourishes and innovation thrives.

Consider, for a moment, the wonder of a child's imagination—the boundless creativity, the uninhibited curiosity, the endless possibilities. Children are natural-born idea generators, unencumbered by the constraints of logic or convention. They see the world through fresh eyes, where every object is a potential source of inspiration, every moment an opportunity for discovery. As we grow older, however, our minds become cluttered with the debris of daily life—responsibilities, obligations, distractions. Yet, within each of us lies the spark of creativity, waiting to be reignited, waiting to illuminate the world with its brilliance.

So, how can we tap into this reservoir of creative potential and unleash the power of our ideas? It begins with a shift in mindset—a willingness to embrace uncertainty, to question the status quo, to explore the unknown. It's about cultivating a sense of wonder and curiosity, and nurturing our innate capacity for imagination and innovation. By creating an environment that nurtures creativity, we can unlock the full potential of our minds and unleash a torrent of ideas that have the power to transform our lives and the world around us.

As we journey deeper into the psychology of ideas, let us pause to reflect on the deep impact they have on our perception of reality. From the simple act of observing a sunset to the complex process of solving a mathematical equation, ideas are the invisible threads that connect us to the world and to each other. They are the engines of innovation, the catalysts of change, and the essence of what it means to be human. So, the next time you find yourself lost in thought, thinking the mysteries of the universe, think of that ideas are the fuel that powers the journey of discovery and the spark that ignites the flame of imagination. Adopt them, nurture them, and watch as they illuminate the path to a brighter, more beautiful world.

Secrets of Creativity

Creativity is not some mystical gift bestowed upon a chosen few, but rather a complex interplay of cognitive processes within the brain. Neuroscientists have uncovered that creativity involves multiple regions of the brain working together in harmony, from the prefrontal cortex responsible for executive functions like decision-making and problem-solving, to the limbic system associated with emotions and motivation.

But what truly ignites the spark of creativity? Research suggests that the brain operates most creatively when it's in a state of relaxed alertness, known as the alpha state. This state of mind allows for spontaneous connections to form between seemingly unrelated ideas, leading to novel insights and breakthrough innovations. So, the next time you find yourself struggling to come up with a creative solution, try taking a step back, relaxing your mind, and allowing your thoughts to flow freely.

But creativity isn't just about generating ideas; it's also about selecting and refining the most promising ones. This process involves a delicate balance of divergent thinking, where we explore a wide range of possibilities, and convergent thinking, where we focus on narrowing down and developing the best ideas. By mastering this balance, we can transform raw creativity into actionable plans and projects that have the power to change the world.

So, how can we cultivate our creative abilities and tap into the boundless potential of our minds? One key is to adopt a growth mindset, recognizing that creativity is a skill that can be developed and nurtured over time. By adopting a curious and open-minded approach to life, we can expose ourselves to new experiences, ideas, and perspectives that fuel our creative spark.

Another crucial factor in fostering creativity is creating an environment that supports innovation and experimentation. Whether it's a physical space conducive to collaboration and brainstorming or a culture that encourages risk-taking and learning from failure, the right conditions can nurture creativity and unleash its full power.

In a world marked by rapid change and uncertainty, the ability to think creatively and generate innovative solutions is the key to adapting, thriving, and shaping a brighter future for ourselves and generations to come. So, let's understand the science behind ideas, unlock our creative potential, and dare to imagine the possibilities that lie ahead.

Exploring the Neuroscience of Creativity

Imagine your brain as a vast universe, with billions of neurons firing and connecting in intricate patterns. When we engage in creative thinking, this neural network lights up like a constellation, sparking new connections and ideas. Neuroscientists have used advanced imaging techniques like functional magnetic resonance imaging (fMRI) to observe this process in action, revealing the areas of the brain responsible for creativity.

One key region of interest is the prefrontal cortex, often dubbed the brain's "CEO" for its role in executive functions like planning, decision-making, and—yes, you guessed it—creativity. But creativity isn't just a solo act; it's a team effort that involves multiple brain regions working in harmony. The default mode network, responsible for mind-wandering and introspection, also plays a crucial role in creative thinking, allowing ideas to bubble up from our subconscious.

Investigating the Factors that Influence Idea Generation and Innovation

But what factors influence our ability to generate ideas and innovate? It turns out that creativity is a complex interplay of nature and nurture, influenced by a wide range of factors. From genetic predispositions to environmental stimuli, our brains are constantly shaped by our experiences and surroundings.

One factor that significantly impacts idea generation is our mindset. Research has shown that adopting a growth mindset—believing that our abilities can be developed through effort and perseverance—can boost creative thinking. Similarly, our environment plays a crucial role in stimulating creativity.

But perhaps the most powerful catalyst for innovation is diversity. When we surround ourselves with people from different backgrounds, cultures, and perspectives, we open ourselves up to a rich tapestry of ideas and insights. Collaboration becomes the secret sauce of creativity, as diverse teams bring together a multitude of perspectives to tackle complex problems and drive innovation forward.

As we go deeper into the science behind ideas, we begin to see creativity not as a mysterious gift bestowed upon the chosen few, but as a universal human trait waiting to be nurtured and cultivated. By understanding the neuroscience of creativity and the factors that influence idea generation, we can unlock our full creative potential and harness the power of ideas to shape a brighter future for ourselves and the world around us.

Idea Power

Ideas stand as the architects of our reality, shaping our world with their transformative potential. From the humblest beginnings to the grandest achievements, every monumental leap forward begins with a spark of inspiration—a flicker of possibility that ignites the imagination and drives us into uncharted territories of innovation and discovery.

Sara Blakely, a woman with a simple idea, revolutionized an entire industry. Frustrated by the lack of comfortable undergarments that wouldn't show under her white pants, Sara had a lightbulb moment: what if she could create a better solution herself? Armed with little more than a pair of scissors and a lot of determination, Sara set out to design the perfect undergarment—one that would slim and shape without sacrificing comfort. The result? Spanx, a multi-million-dollar empire that transformed the way women everywhere feel and look in their clothes.

Sara's story is a proof to the power of ideas to change lives, challenge conventions, and defy limitations. But connecting the power of ideas is about more than just having a stroke of genius—it's about nurturing that spark of inspiration and fanning it into flames of innovation. It's about nuturing a mindset of creativity, curiosity, and courage that allows us to see beyond the status quo and envision a world that is richer, brighter, and more fulfilling than the one we know.

So, how do we unleash the power of ideas in our own lives? It starts with adopting the belief that every idea, no matter how small or seemingly insignificant, has the potential to make a difference. It's about being open to new possibilities, exploring uncharted territories, and daring to dream big. It's about surrounding ourselves with diverse perspectives, collaborating with others, and drawing inspiration from the world around us.

But perhaps most importantly, harnessing the power of ideas is about taking action. It's about rolling up our sleeves, diving headfirst into the unknown, and daring to fail in pursuit of something greater. Because it's in the process of trial and error, experimentation and iteration, that ideas truly come to life and change the world.

So, as you journey through life, think of the words of Sara Blakely and countless other innovators who have dared to dream the impossible: "Don't be intimidated by what you don't know. That can be your greatest strength and ensure that you do things differently from everyone else." Tap into the power of your ideas, and who knows? You just might change the world.

Cultivating a Creative Mindset

In the world of ideas, creativity reigns supreme. It's the spark that ignites innovation, the fuel that drives progress, and the cornerstone of success. But how do we cultivate a creative mindset—one that allows us to tap into our full potential and unleash the power of our ideas?

Meet Elon Musk, the visionary entrepreneur behind companies like Tesla, SpaceX, and Neuralink. From a young age, Musk displayed a voracious appetite for learning and a boundless imagination that knew no bounds. But it wasn't until later in life that he truly adopted the power of creativity as a driving force in his endeavors.

As Musk began his entrepreneurial journey, he encountered countless challenges and setbacks, from failed business ventures to near bankruptcy. But instead of succumbing to defeat, Musk viewed each obstacle as an opportunity to innovate and push the boundaries of what was possible. His secret? A relentless commitment to build a creative mindset.

For Musk, creativity wasn't just about thinking outside the box—it was about shattering the box altogether. He encouraged his teams to embrace bold ideas, challenge conventional wisdom, and push past their comfort zones in pursuit of greatness. This spirit of audacity and innovation became the hallmark of Musk's companies, driving breakthroughs in electric vehicles, space exploration, and beyond.

But developing a creative mindset isn't just about big ideas and grand visions—it's also about fostering a culture of experimentation, collaboration, and open-mindedness. Musk understood the importance of surrounding himself with diverse perspectives and challenging his own assumptions, which ultimately fueled his success.

So, how can we cultivate a creative mindset in our own lives? It starts with adopting curiosity and adopting failure as opportunities for growth. Instead of fearing mistakes, we should view them as stepping stones on the path to innovation. We should seek out new experiences, engage with different ideas and perspectives, and never stop asking questions.

Moreover, we must create an environment that nurtures creativity, whether it's through regular brainstorming sessions, interdisciplinary collaboration, or simply carving out time for reflection and ideation. By fostering a culture of creativity in our personal and professional lives, we can unlock new possibilities, overcome obstacles, and unleash the full potential of our ideas.

Therefore, developing a creative mindset isn't just a luxury—it's a necessity in today's fast-paced, ever-changing world. By following in the footsteps of visionaries like Elon Musk and adopting creativity as a guiding principle, we can tap into our innate potential, transform challenges into opportunities, and shape a brighter future for ourselves and generations to come. So, let's dare to dream big, think boldly, and unleash the power of our ideas to change the world.

In a world teeming with ideas, creativity is the spark that ignites innovation, fuels progress, and transforms the ordinary into the extraordinary. Yet, for many of us, tapping into our creative potential can feel like searching for a needle in a haystack. How do we unlock the door to our imagination and unleash our creative prowess? Let's explore.

Unlocking Your Creative Potential

Consider the story of Apple, the tech giant renowned for its groundbreaking products and visionary design. Behind the sleek iPhones and iconic MacBooks lies a culture of innovation fostered by the late Steve Jobs. Jobs understood the power of creativity and believed that every individual possessed the ability to think differently. He encouraged his team to push boundaries, take risks, and challenge conventional thinking. By nurturing a culture that celebrated creativity and embraced diversity of thought, Apple revolutionized industries and changed the way we interact with technology.

Similarly, LEGO, the beloved toy company, has built an empire on the foundation of creativity and imagination. From humble beginnings in a

Danish carpenter's workshop to becoming one of the world's most beloved brands, LEGO has inspired generations of builders and dreamers. By fostering a culture of play, experimentation, and limitless possibility, LEGO empowers children and adults alike to unleash their creativity and build their own worlds brick by brick.

Overcoming Mental Blocks and Limiting Beliefs

Despite the endless potential within us, many of us grapple with mental blocks and limiting beliefs that stifle our creativity. We may fear failure, doubt our abilities, or succumb to the pressure to conform. But the truth is, creativity thrives in the face of adversity.

The iconic sportswear brand, Nike's famous slogan, "Just Do It," symbolizes the spirit of creativity and resilience. Co-founder Phil Knight once said, "The only way to deal with fear is to stare it down. You can't let it paralyze you." Nike's success is a testimony to the power of perseverance and the willingness to push past obstacles in pursuit of greatness.

Similarly, Starbucks, the global coffee giant, has overcome its fair share of challenges on the road to success. From humble beginnings in a single Seattle café to a ubiquitous presence on street corners around the world, Starbucks has thrived by embracing innovation and adapting to change. By staying true to its core values of quality, community, and creativity, Starbucks has transformed the coffee industry and redefined the café experience for millions.

Finally, developing a creative mindset is not just about generating ideas; it's about embracing a way of thinking that empowers us to see the world through new eyes, explore uncharted territory, and challenge the status quo. So, dare to dream, dare to create, and dare to be different. Your creative journey starts now.

Idea Generation Techniques

Idea generation is similar to mining for precious gems—it requires patience, skill, and a keen eye for potential. In this chapter, we delve into various techniques for igniting the spark of inspiration and uncovering innovative ideas that have the potential to transform lives and industries.

1. Brainstorming:

A group of individuals gathered around a table, tossing around ideas like a game of catch. This is brainstorming—a tried-and-true technique for generating a flood of ideas in a short amount of time. One notable example of successful brainstorming comes from the world of tech giant Google. The company's "20% time" policy allows employees to spend a fifth of their workweek pursuing passion projects, leading to innovations such as Gmail and Google Maps.

2. Mind Mapping:

Imagine your thoughts as branches on a tree, each connected to a central idea. This is the essence of mind mapping—a visual technique for organizing thoughts and generating new connections. One company that has leveraged mind mapping to great effect is Disney. Walt Disney himself was known for sketching out elaborate mind maps to brainstorm story ideas for beloved classics like "Snow White" and "Cinderella."

3. SCAMPER Technique:

SCAMPER is more than just a playful acronym—it's a powerful tool for sparking creativity by prompting you to ask questions and explore different angles of a problem. Take Coca-Cola, for example. When faced with declining sales in the 1980s, the company applied the SCAMPER technique to reinvent their flagship product, resulting in the introduction of Diet Coke—a groundbreaking innovation that revitalized the brand.

4. Reverse Thinking:

Sometimes, the best way to solve a problem is to turn it on its head. Reverse thinking encourages you to challenge assumptions and explore unconventional solutions. A prime example of this approach can be found in Airbnb's early days. When founders Brian Chesky and Joe Gebbia struggled to attract users to their platform, they turned to reverse thinking, offering professional photoshoots to hosts to improve the quality of their listings—an idea that ultimately helped Airbnb to success.

5. Provocation:

Provocation is about pushing boundaries and daring to think outside the box. It involves deliberately provoking thoughts and ideas that challenge the status quo. One company that has mastered the art of provocation is Tesla. By boldly challenging the automotive industry with electric vehicles and autonomous driving technology, Tesla has disrupted the market and reshaped the future of transportation.

6. Random Stimulus:

Sometimes, inspiration strikes when you least expect it. Random stimulus techniques involve exposing yourself to diverse inputs and letting your mind make unexpected connections. Take the case of Twitter, for instance. The idea for the microblogging platform came to co-founder Jack Dorsey while he was stuck in traffic, thinking the concept of status updates and real-time communication—a random stimulus that led to a billion-dollar idea.

7. Design Thinking: Design thinking is more than just a method—it's a mindset, a philosophy, a way of approaching problems with empathy and creativity. It involves empathizing with users, defining problems, ideating solutions, prototyping ideas, and testing them in real-world scenarios. Take Airbnb, for instance. The company used design thinking principles to reimagine the travel experience, creating a platform that allows people to book unique accommodations and connect with local hosts around the world. By putting the needs of travelers at the forefront of their design process, Airbnb disrupted the hospitality industry and unlocked new possibilities for exploration and connection.

8. Problem-Solving Frameworks: When faced with a challenge, it can be helpful to employ

structured problem-solving frameworks to guide the ideation process. One such framework is the "Five Whys," which involves asking "why" five times to uncover the root cause of a problem and generate potential solutions. Toyota, the Japanese automotive manufacturer, is known for using the Five Whys technique to drive continuous improvement and innovation. By digging deep to understand the underlying causes of issues, Toyota has been able to develop innovative solutions that enhance quality, efficiency, and safety across its operations.

These methods are just the tip of the iceberg. Whether you're brainstorming with a team, mind mapping solo, or reverse engineering your favorite products, the key is to embrace curiosity, creativity, and collaboration. So, what method will you choose to unlock your next big idea? The possibilities are endless—let your imagination soar!

Developing Ideas

One of the most crucial stages in the journey of harnessing the power of ideas is refining and developing them into actionable plans. It's like shaping rough stones into sparkling gems, where each cut and polish reveals the true brilliance within. Let's dive into this transformative process and explore some tools and techniques that can turn raw ideas into shining beacons of innovation.

1. Evaluating and Selecting Promising Ideas

Imagine you're standing in front of a buffet table overflowing with delicious dishes. You can't possibly taste everything, so you have to choose wisely. Similarly, when refining ideas, you need to evaluate and select the most promising ones to pursue further.

Apple is renowned for its product innovation, but not every idea makes it to market. Steve Jobs famously implemented a "top 100" meeting where the best ideas were discussed and prioritized, ensuring that only the most promising concepts moved forward.

2. Developing Ideas into Actionable Plans and Projects

Once you've identified your top ideas, it's time to roll up your sleeves and start developing them into actionable plans and projects. This involves finding out the details, setting goals, and creating a roadmap for implementation.

Google encourages employees to spend 20% of their time working on passion projects. This initiative has led to the development of groundbreaking products like Gmail and Google Maps, demonstrating the power of giving ideas time and space to grow.

3. Iterative Prototyping and Testing

Innovation is rarely a linear process; it's more like a series of experiments where each iteration brings you closer to perfection. Prototyping and testing allow you to gather feedback, refine your ideas, and make improvements along the way.

Amazon's customer review system is a prime example of iterative prototyping. By allowing customers to provide feedback on products, Amazon continuously refines its offerings based on user input, resulting in a more satisfying shopping experience for everyone.

4. Collaborative Problem-Solving

Two heads are better than one, and when it comes to refining ideas, collaboration can lead to breakthroughs. By bringing together diverse perspectives and skill sets, teams can tackle complex problems and generate innovative solutions.

LEGO's Ideas platform allows fans to submit their own designs for new LEGO sets. Users vote on their favorite designs, and if a project receives enough support, LEGO considers producing it as an official set. This collaborative approach has resulted in the creation of fan-favorite sets like the LEGO NASA Apollo Saturn V.

5. Accepting Failure as a Learning Opportunity

Finally, it's essential to accept failure as a natural part of the refining process. Not every idea will succeed on the first try, but each failure brings valuable lessons that can inform future iterations and ultimately lead to success.

Before perfecting his revolutionary vacuum cleaner, James Dyson famously built 5,126 prototypes that didn't work. Instead of seeing these failures as setbacks, Dyson embraced them as opportunities for learning and refinement, ultimately leading to the creation of the Dyson Cyclone vacuum, which revolutionized the industry.

Refining and developing the ideas is where the magic happens. By evaluating, developing, iterating, collaborating, and adopting failure, you can transform raw ideas into game-changing innovations that have the potential to shape the world. So, roll up your sleeves, sharpen your pencils, and get ready to refine your ideas into greatness. The world is waiting for your brilliance to shine.

Applying Ideas

Ideas are the threads that weave together innovation, progress, and transformation. They are the sparks of creativity that ignite revolutions, disrupt industries, and shape the course of history. But what is it about ideas that make them so potent, so influential, and so utterly transformative?

In the late 1970s, two college dropouts, Steve Jobs and Steve Wozniak, had a vision—to bring the power of computing to the masses. Their idea gave birth to the Apple I, a revolutionary personal computer that paved the way for a new era of technology. Fast forward to the present day, and Apple has become synonymous with innovation, known for its iconic products like the iPhone, iPad, and MacBook. What began as a simple idea in a garage has blossomed into a global empire, forever changing the way we live, work, and communicate.

But it's not just tech giants like Apple that harness the power of ideas to drive change. Airbnb is a startup that disrupted the hospitality industry with its simple yet revolutionary idea: connecting travelers with unique and affordable accommodations around the world. Founded in 2008 by Brian Chesky, Joe Gebbia, and Nathan Blecharczyk, Airbnb began as a way for the founders to make ends meet by renting out air mattresses in their San Francisco apartment. Little did they know, their idea would revolutionize the way people travel, transforming the hospitality industry and empowering millions of hosts and guests worldwide.

What these stories teach us is that ideas have the power to transcend boundaries, break down barriers, and reshape the world in profound ways. But how can we apply the power of ideas in our own lives, businesses, and communities?

Firstly, we must cultivate a mindset of curiosity, exploration, and open-mindedness. Ideas often emerge when we least expect them, but they are more likely to flourish in an environment where creativity is nurtured and encouraged. Take Google, for example—a company known for its culture of innovation and experimentation. From its famous "20% time" policy that allows employees to pursue passion projects to its colorful and collaborative workspaces, Google fosters an environment where ideas can thrive and flourish.

Secondly, we must be willing to take risks, accept failure, and learn from our mistakes. Not every idea will be a success, but every failure is an opportunity to learn, grow, and refine our thinking. Consider the story of Thomas Edison, who famously said, "I have not failed. I've just found 10,000 ways that won't work" while inventing the light bulb. Edison's perseverance and willingness to embrace failure ultimately led to one of the most transformative inventions in history—an idea that illuminated the world and changed the course of human civilization.

Finally, we must be mindful of the impact our ideas have on the world around us. Ideas have the power to uplift and empower, but they also have the power to harm and divide. As we apply the power of ideas in our own lives and businesses, let us strive to create positive change, foster inclusivity, and leave a lasting legacy of innovation and inspiration for future generations.

To wrap up, the power of ideas is a force to be counted with—a force that has the potential to transform lives, businesses, and the world. By developing a mindset of creativity, accepting failure as a stepping stone to success, and harnessing the power of our ideas for good, we can unlock a world of infinite possibilities and create a brighter future for all. So let us dare to dream, dare to innovate, and dare to change the world—one idea at a time.

Daily Implementation

We encounter countless opportunities to tap into the power of ideas, whether it's solving a problem at work, finding a creative solution to a household task, or simply navigating the challenges of daily life. Let's deep dive to know how incorporating creative thinking into our daily tasks and using ideas to overcome challenges can lead to remarkable outcomes.

Incorporating Creative Thinking into Everyday Tasks and Activities

LEGO is the iconic toy company beloved by children and adults alike. When LEGO faced declining sales in the early 2000s, they knew they needed to shake things up. Instead of sticking to their traditional business model, they decided to think outside the box. They introduced LEGO Ideas, a platform that allows fans to submit their own designs for new LEGO sets. This simple idea not only reinvigorated the brand but also tapped into the creativity of LEGO enthusiasts worldwide. By adopting creative thinking and involving their customers in the product development process, LEGO transformed their business and created a vibrant community of loyal fans.

Similarly, Starbucks, the global coffee giant, revolutionized the way we think about coffee shops by incorporating creative thinking into every aspect of their business. From the cozy ambiance of their stores to the innovative drinks on their menu, Starbucks is constantly pushing the boundaries of what a coffee shop can be. One of their most successful ideas was the introduction of the Starbucks Rewards program, which rewards loyal customers with exclusive perks and discounts. This simple idea not only incentivized repeat business but also fostered a sense of belonging and community among Starbucks customers worldwide.

Using Ideas to Solve Problems and Overcome Challenges

Now, let's turn our attention to how ideas can be used to solve problems and overcome challenges in our daily lives. Take the story of Airbnb, the online marketplace for short-term lodging. When founders Brian Chesky and Joe Gebbia were struggling to pay rent on their San Francisco apartment, they came up with a creative solution: renting out air mattresses in their living room to travelers attending a local conference. This simple idea eventually evolved into Airbnb, a multi-billion-dollar company that has revolutionized the hospitality industry. By thinking outside the box and turning their problem into an opportunity, Chesky and Gebbia not only solved their immediate financial woes but also created a platform that connects millions of travelers with unique and affordable accommodations around the world.

Similarly, Dropbox, the cloud storage service, was born out of a simple idea to solve a common problem. Founder Drew Houston often found himself forgetting his USB drive and struggling to access files across multiple devices. To address this frustration, he came up with the idea for Dropbox—a seamless way to store, sync, and share files online. This innovative solution not only solved Houston's problem but also revolutionized the way we store and access data in the digital age. Today, Dropbox is used by millions of individuals and businesses worldwide, demonstrating the power of a single idea to transform an industry.

Incorporating creative thinking into everyday tasks and using ideas to solve problems and overcome challenges can lead to remarkable outcomes, as demonstrated by the stories of LEGO, Starbucks, Airbnb, and Dropbox. By embracing creativity, thinking outside the box, and daring to pursue new ideas, we can unlock endless possibilities in our own lives and create positive change in the world around us.

Impactful Ideas

Nothing speaks louder than real-world examples of transformative change brought about by ingenious thinking. Let's deep dive into the stories of renowned brands whose innovative ideas have not only reshaped industries but also left an indelible mark on the lives of people worldwide.

Starbucks: Brewing a Global Coffee Culture

A small coffee shop envisioned something grander than just serving a morning pick-me-up. Starbucks, with its humble beginnings in 1971, transformed the way the world savors coffee. By creating a welcoming ambiance and elevating the coffee-drinking experience, Starbucks revolutionized the notion of a café. Today, Starbucks isn't just a coffee chain; it's a cultural phenomenon, fostering community connections and redefining the concept of a third place. Its innovative idea didn't just sell coffee; it sold an experience—a lifestyle that millions around the globe now embrace.

Dollar Shave Club: Disrupting the Goliaths of Grooming

In an industry dominated by behemoths, Dollar Shave Club dared to challenge the status quo with a simple yet revolutionary idea: affordable, high-quality razors delivered right to your doorstep. By bypassing traditional retail channels and embracing a subscription-based model, Dollar Shave Club democratized grooming, making it accessible to the masses. With witty marketing campaigns and a focus on customer experience, the brand quickly carved out a niche in the competitive landscape, disrupting the giants of grooming and proving that innovative ideas can topple even the most entrenched incumbents.

Tesla: Driving the Future of Transportation

When Elon Musk set out to revolutionize the automotive industry, many doubted the feasibility of his vision. Yet, with Tesla Motors, Musk turned skeptics into believers, showcasing the power of disruptive innovation. By marrying cutting-edge technology with sustainable energy solutions, Tesla not only redefined the concept of an electric vehicle but also challenged conventional notions of what a car could be. With sleek designs, unparalleled performance, and a commitment to sustainability, Tesla has not only changed the way we think about transportation but also inspired a global movement towards a greener, more sustainable future.

Netflix: Rewriting the Script on Entertainment

In the age of blockbuster films and primetime television, Netflix dared to reimagine the way we consume entertainment. With its groundbreaking idea of streaming content directly to viewers' homes, Netflix disrupted the traditional media landscape, forever altering the way we watch movies and TV shows. By leveraging data analytics to personalize recommendations and investing in original content production, Netflix transformed itself from a DVD rental service to a global entertainment powerhouse. Its innovative idea didn't just disrupt an industry; it ushered in a new era of on-demand, binge-worthy entertainment, forever changing the way we unwind and escape into the world of storytelling.

These stories of Starbucks, Dollar Shave Club, Tesla, and Netflix inspire us to think beyond the confines of the status quo, to challenge norms, and to dare to dream big. Because, as these brands have shown, it's often those bold, game-changing ideas that have the power to transform not only industries but also the world around us.

Life-Changing Ideas

Great ideas have the power to change lives, transforming the way we live, work, and interact with the world around us. Let's explore some of these transformative ideas in simple language:

The Printing Press: In the 15th century, Johannes Gutenberg invented the printing press, revolutionizing the way information was disseminated. Before the printing press, books were copied by hand, making them rare and expensive. With the advent of the printing press, books became more accessible, leading to an explosion of knowledge and the spread of literacy.

The Internet: In the late 20th century, the internet changed the world forever. Originally developed as a way for scientists to communicate, the internet evolved into a global network that connects billions of people around the world. It has transformed how we communicate, shop, learn, and work, making information more accessible than ever before.

The Wheel: The invention of the wheel is one of humanity's greatest achievements. While the exact date of its invention is unknown, the wheel revolutionized transportation, allowing people to travel faster and carry heavier loads. It paved the way for the development of vehicles, carts, and other forms of transportation that have shaped the course of history.

The Scientific Method: The scientific method, developed during the Renaissance, transformed the way we understand the world. It is a systematic approach to inquiry that involves making observations, forming hypotheses, conducting experiments, and analyzing data. The scientific method has led to countless discoveries and advancements in fields such as medicine, technology, and engineering.

Democracy: Democracy, the system of government in which power is vested in the people, has had a profound impact on human history. Ancient civilizations such as Athens and Rome practiced forms of democracy, but it wasn't until the Enlightenment that democratic principles were fully embraced. Today, democracy is the most widely practiced form of government in the world, providing people with a voice in their governance.

The Steam Engine: The steam engine, invented during the Industrial Revolution, transformed society by powering machinery and transportation. It enabled factories to mass-produce goods, leading to the rise of industry and urbanization. The steam engine also revolutionized transportation, making it faster and more efficient than ever before.

Vaccines: Vaccines are one of the greatest medical innovations in history. They work by stimulating the immune system to produce antibodies against specific diseases, preventing infection and the spread of illness. Vaccines have eradicated smallpox, nearly eliminated diseases like polio and measles, and saved millions of lives around the world.

The Declaration of Independence: The Declaration of Independence, written by Thomas Jefferson in 1776, proclaimed the United States' independence from British rule and laid out the principles of liberty and equality. It inspired revolutions around the world and served as a blueprint for future democracies.

The Green Revolution: The Green Revolution, which began in the mid-20th century, transformed agriculture and food production. Through the use of advanced technologies such as high-yield crop varieties, fertilizers, and pesticides, the Green Revolution increased food production, alleviated hunger, and improved living standards for millions of people.

The Universal Declaration of Human Rights: Adopted by the United Nations General Assembly in 1948, the Universal Declaration of Human Rights is a milestone document that proclaims the rights and freedoms to which all people are entitled. It has inspired laws and constitutions around the world and serves as a beacon of hope for the advancement of human rights and dignity.

Businesses are constantly seeking innovative ideas to stay ahead of the competition and thrive in a dynamic marketplace. These ideas have the power to transform the way companies operate, drive growth, and create lasting impact. Let's explore some great ideas that have the potential to revolutionize businesses -

Digital Transformation: Adopting digital technologies is essential for businesses to stay relevant and competitive in the digital age. From implementing cloud computing and data analytics to developing mobile apps and e-commerce platforms, leveraging digital tools can streamline processes, enhance customer experiences, and unlock new revenue streams.

Customer-Centricity: Putting customers at the center of everything they do is a game-changer for businesses. By understanding customer needs, preferences, and pain points, companies can tailor their products, services, and marketing efforts to provide personalized experiences that resonate with their target audience and foster loyalty.

Innovative Product Development: Developing innovative products that address unmet needs or solve pressing problems is key to driving business growth. Whether it's introducing groundbreaking technologies, creating eco-friendly solutions, or reimagining traditional products with a modern twist, innovation is the lifeblood of successful businesses.

Agile Methodology: Adopting agile methodologies allows businesses to adapt quickly to changing market conditions and customer demands. By breaking projects into smaller, manageable tasks and iterating based on feedback, teams can deliver value more efficiently, reduce time-to-market, and foster a culture of continuous improvement.

Strategic Partnerships: Collaborating with strategic partners can open doors to new markets, resources, and opportunities for businesses. Whether it's forming alliances with complementary businesses, partnering with industry leaders, or engaging in joint ventures, strategic partnerships can accelerate growth and drive innovation.

Employee Empowerment: Empowering employees to take ownership of their work and contribute ideas fosters a culture of innovation and collaboration within organizations. By providing training, mentorship, and autonomy, businesses can unleash the creative potential of their workforce and drive meaningful change from within.

Sustainability Initiatives: Incorporating sustainability into business practices is not only good for the planet but also for the bottom line. From reducing carbon emissions and minimizing waste to sourcing ethically and promoting corporate social responsibility, businesses can attract environmentally-conscious consumers, enhance brand reputation, and create long-term value.

Data-Driven Decision Making: Leveraging data and analytics to inform decision-making is critical for businesses to gain insights, identify trends, and make informed strategic choices. By collecting and analyzing data from various sources, businesses can optimize operations, personalize marketing campaigns, and drive business performance.

Disruptive Business Models: Disruptive business models have the potential to reshape entire industries and create new market opportunities. Whether it's subscription-based services, sharing economies, or peer-to-peer marketplaces, businesses that challenge the status quo and embrace innovation can gain a competitive edge and thrive in a rapidly changing landscape.

Continuous Learning and Adaptation: In a world where change is constant, businesses must embrace a culture of continuous learning and adaptation. By staying abreast of industry trends, adopting new technologies, and developing a growth mindset among employees, businesses can future-proof themselves and remain agile and resilient in the face of uncertainty.

These are just a few examples of great ideas that have changed the course of history and transformed the lives of people around the world. From inventions and innovations to principles and declarations, these ideas have left an indelible mark on humanity, shaping the world we live in today.

Business-Leveraging Ideas

One remarkable example of how a single idea can push a business to new heights is the success story of Flipkart in India. Founded in 2007 by Sachin Bansal and Binny Bansal, Flipkart started as an online bookstore, aiming to offer a convenient alternative to traditional brick-and-mortar bookstores. However, the founders quickly realized the potential of e-commerce and expanded their product offerings to include a wide range of categories, from electronics to fashion.

The one idea that transformed Flipkart's path was introducing cash-on-delivery (COD) as a payment option. In a country where online payments were not widely adopted due to concerns about security and trust, COD provided customers with the assurance of paying only upon receiving their orders. This simple yet innovative idea addressed a major barrier to online shopping in India and opened up a vast untapped market of customers who were previously hesitant to shop online.

The introduction of COD not only boosted Flipkart's sales but also played a crucial role in establishing trust and credibility among Indian consumers. It allowed Flipkart to reach customers in smaller towns and cities where access to digital payment methods was limited, thus democratizing e-commerce and making online shopping accessible to a wider audience.

As Flipkart continued to innovate and adapt to the evolving needs of its customers, it solidified its position as India's leading e-commerce platform. The success of Flipkart's COD initiative demonstrated the transformative power of a single idea in driving business growth and market expansion in the Indian context. It serves as a testament to the importance of understanding local dynamics and leveraging innovative solutions to overcome unique challenges in emerging markets like India.

Another example of a single idea transforming a business in the Indian market is the success story of Paytm. Founded in 2010 by Vijay Shekhar Sharma, Paytm initially started as a mobile recharge and bill payment platform. However, the company's breakthrough moment came with the introduction of digital wallets, allowing users to make cashless transactions for a wide range of services, including mobile recharges, bill payments, and online shopping.

Paytm's digital wallet revolutionized the way Indians conducted financial transactions, particularly in a country where cash was king. With the demonetization drive in 2016, which led to a severe shortage of physical currency, Paytm emerged as a lifeline for millions of Indians seeking a convenient and secure alternative to cash. The company's digital wallet saw a surge in adoption as people turned to digital payments for their everyday needs.

The introduction of digital wallets not only drove Paytm's growth but also played a significant role in advancing India's digital economy. It accelerated the adoption of cashless transactions across various sectors, including retail, transportation, and entertainment, contributing to the government's vision of a less-cash society.

Another notable example is Zomato, an online food delivery and restaurant discovery platform. Founded in 2008 by Deepinder Goyal and Pankaj Chaddah, Zomato initially started as a restaurant review website. However, the company's transformational idea came with the introduction of online food delivery services.

Recognizing the growing demand for convenient food delivery options, Zomato diversified its business model to include online ordering and food delivery services. This strategic pivot allowed Zomato to tap into the growing food delivery market in India, offering customers a wide selection of cuisines delivered right to their doorstep.

Zomato's foray into online food delivery not only expanded its revenue streams but also positioned the company as a dominant player in India's competitive food delivery market. The platform's seamless ordering experience, extensive restaurant network, and timely delivery services have made it a preferred choice for millions of customers seeking hassle-free dining experiences.

Conclusion

As we draw to a close on our journey through "The Power of Ideas," it's clear that ideas have the remarkable ability to transform lives in ways both big and small. This book has been about unlocking the immense potential that ideas hold. We've explored how ideas can spark change, foster innovation, drive success, and ultimately shape our world. Now it's time to reflect on the deep impact that ideas have had on shaping the world around us and empowering lives. Let's highlight some key takeaways and how you can apply them to your life.

Key Takeaways

1. Ideas Are the Seeds of Change

Throughout this book, we've seen how a single idea can transform lives, businesses, and even societies. Whether it's a groundbreaking invention, a revolutionary business model, or a simple yet powerful change in perspective, ideas are the starting point of all progress.

2. Creativity and Innovation Go Hand in Hand

Innovation stems from creativity. By nurturing your creative thinking, you can come up with innovative solutions to problems. This involves being open to new experiences, questioning the status quo, and being willing to take risks.

3. Execution is Key

Having a great idea is just the beginning. Turning that idea into reality requires planning, persistence, and action. We've discussed various strategies to move from ideation to execution, emphasizing the importance of taking consistent, deliberate steps towards your goals.

4. Collaboration Amplifies Impact

Ideas flourish when they are shared and developed collaboratively. Building a network of supportive, like-minded individuals can provide new insights, resources, and motivation. Working together can take your ideas further than you could alone.

5. Adaptability is Crucial

The journey from idea to impact is rarely straightforward. Flexibility and adaptability are essential. Being able to pivot, refine, and adjust your ideas in response to feedback and changing circumstances can make the difference between success and failure.

6. Persistence Pays Off

Many of the world's greatest ideas took time to develop and required persistence to overcome obstacles. Staying committed to your vision, even in the face of setbacks, is vital. The stories we've explored highlight the power of perseverance.

Moving Forward

1. Commit to Continuous Learning

The world is constantly changing, and so should your ideas. Commit to lifelong learning. Read widely, seek out new experiences, and stay curious. The more you learn, the more raw material you have to generate innovative ideas.

2. Apply What You've Learned

Start putting the strategies and concepts from this book into practice. Begin with small steps. Identify an idea you've been nurturing and take the first step towards making it a reality. Use the tools and frameworks discussed to refine and execute your idea.

3. Seek Out Like-minded Individuals

Find a community or network where you can share your ideas and collaborate with others. This could be a local meet-up group, an online forum, or a professional organization. Surrounding yourself with creative, supportive people can provide the inspiration and feedback you need.

4. Stay Resilient

Understand that the path from idea to impact will have its challenges. There will be setbacks and obstacles. Use these moments as opportunities to learn and grow. Stay resilient and keep pushing forward.

5. Celebrate Your Wins

Along the way, take time to celebrate your achievements, no matter how small. Acknowledge your progress and use it as motivation to keep going. Celebrating your wins helps maintain your momentum and keeps you focused on your goals.

6. Reflect and Refine

Regularly take time to reflect on your progress. Assess what's working and what isn't. Be willing to adjust your approach as needed. Reflection and refinement are key components of the creative and innovative process.

A Commitment to Action

The power of ideas is not just a concept; it's a call to action. By now, you understand the potential within you to generate and implement powerful ideas. The next step is to commit to using that potential. Make a promise to yourself to take action on your ideas. Whether it's a personal project, a business venture, or a community initiative, start today. Use the insights and strategies you've gained to bring your ideas to life.

As you move forward, keep this book as a resource and a reminder of the power within you. Revisit the concepts and stories when you need inspiration or guidance. Share what you've learned with others and be a source of inspiration and support for those around you.

In a world that's constantly evolving, your ideas can be the spark that drives positive change. The journey won't always be easy, but it will be worthwhile. Your ideas have the power to shape your future and make a meaningful impact on the world.

Let us remember that the journey doesn't end here. Ideas are constantly evolving, and there are infinite possibilities waiting to be explored. So, dare to dream big, dare to think boldly, and dare to believe in the power of your ideas to change the world. After all, as history has shown us time and time again, the greatest achievements often begin with a single idea and the courage to pursue it.

So, take that first step. Start brainstorming, planning, and executing. Connect with others, stay adaptable, and persist through challenges. Celebrate your successes and learn from your failures. With each step, you'll be harnessing the incredible power of ideas to create a life filled with purpose, innovation, and success.

Join My Community

https://community.askpndas.com/

www.ingramcontent.com/pod-product-compliance
Lightning Source LLC
Chambersburg PA
CBHW070115230526
45472CB00004B/1269